A FATHER'S LOVE

A FATHER'S

LOVE

Tributes, Praise and Wisdom About Dads and Their Offspring

*Selected by
Peter S. Seymour
Illustrated
by Carl Cassler*

 HALLMARK EDITIONS

A FATHER'S LOVE

Marjorie Holmes:

DADDY CAN FIX IT

Marjorie Holmes' delightful writings have entertained millions of readers all over America. Here she turns her attention to the subject of dads.

Father can fix it. Or Daddy, as little folks call him. Or, as they get older, Pop or Dad.

Whatever his title, there's nothing like that remarkable do-it-yourself but do-it-for-everybody-else male parent.

Often his ingenuity surges to the front even before his offspring arrive, as he fashions a crib, a feeding table. More, today's dad enjoys bathing and feeding his babies sometimes, rocking them, telling them stories. And when they come running in with a broken toy, how many a lucky wife can console, "Don't cry. Wait till Daddy gets home. Your father can fix it."

Daddy can fix it. Anything, everything. Radios, clocks, a bike, a pair of roller skates. A doll, a leaky boat, an eyeless stuffed rabbit. Or those antiques his wife is always dragging home from auction sales. Patiently, cleverly, with glue and tape and nails, and paint and love and imagination — whatever the object, if it's dear to its owner, somehow, some way, he'll devise the means of its salvation.

Father can fix it. Often he will even build it. A playhouse, a picnic table, a fireplace, a wall, a patio in the yard.

Handyman — yes, he's usually that, but more important, he's the family handyman in matters of the heart. Report cards. Budding romances. Times of illness, worry, family strain. That complication in the Cub Scouts, that looming problem at church, at school — don't worry, talk it over with Dad. Dad will analyze the whole thing wisely, come up with the proper solution, make you realize it's not so grave a complication, after all. Or if it proves to be — well, your father will be standing by.

Daddy can fix it. Dad will get it for you. That costume for the play, though it means a trip clear across town. The supplies you need for the bazaar. That last-minute birthday present. Those pretzels and cold drinks for the teen-age party. And regularly, with the car crammed with little folks, groceries at the supermarket on Friday night.

Father can fix it. Find it, get it, pay for it, help you figure it out. Here's to him, bless him — the one who lives at our house, and at yours. The American dad!

Adlai E. Stevenson:

A FATHER'S ROLE

The following is from a speech given by Adlai E. Stevenson, May 25, 1961, before the National Father's Day Committee.

Now it has been said that paternity is a career imposed on you one fine morning without any inquiry as to your fitness for it. That is why there are so many fathers who have children but so few children who have fathers.

Is there truth or cynicism in this remark? A bit of both, I imagine, but far too much of the former for my taste.

It is an all too visible truth that fatherhood is no longer the sacred duty it was once held to be. There are, today, far too many absentee fathers, fathers in name only. Paradoxically, and this is an insight into the nature of contemporary society, they are, in many cases, men whose ability, sense of responsibility and moral integrity outside the home are of the first order.

Apologists for these errant progenitors (in most instances, offenders themselves) have called up a multitude of rationalizations in their defense — two world wars in less than half a century, the pressures of modern urban life, business before pleasure, country before self and other tired old saws.

What nonsense. There is absolutely no excuse for a parent to abdicate his most important duty — the proper raising of his children. No father should be allowed to get away with the cowardly logic which concludes that his only job in the family is to pay for the bacon.

His role is much more grandiose than that. If it is to be properly fulfilled, he should be, in his realm, a man of many faces — an artist, a philosopher, a statesman and, above all, a prolific dispenser of good sense and justice.

But it is vitally important, especially in the early years, that his children see in father a working model of the social order in which, not so many years hence, they will be expected to play a dynamic part.

How can we, the parents, hope to secure a just and rational society if we neglect the development of those very instruments, our children, most necessary for its implementation? What good does it do to conceive grand moral, social or political plans for a better world if the children who will have to live them out fail to see their importance?

In a very real sense, a father's relations with his children should be a microcosmic reflection of their relations with the society in which they live. Through his actions a father must teach his children the intrinsic meaning of the democratic concept—freedom with restraint and the nature of integrity.

Several years ago, at a "Father-and-Son Team of the Year" ceremony held by the National Father's Day Committee, the father was the first to speak and said:

I claim no credit for my son being what he is...people make their own intellectual and moral characters. If he was helped in making his by me... it was he who decided to accept the help. The decision in such matters is finally with ourselves. To say that responsibility begins at home should mean, I think, that it begins — and ends, too — in the individual. Sooner or later he must help himself. There are no alibis.

The son then spoke of his father:

He has been able to move me, to laughter and to tears, for as long as I can remember, both in public and in private — and that's of the greatest importance. For my father has been to me both a public and a private man.

But my experience has reminded me of something that he taught me — not consciously, I'm sure, but as an example. For the extraordinary thing about my father is that his public face and his private face have been the same. He has been the same man to the world as he has been to his family. And that is harder than it sounds.

It is the very definition of integrity, I suppose.

Edward Streeter:

FATHER OF THE BRIDE

Edward Streeter describes in his novel how Mr. Banks manages to get through the wedding ceremony of his daughter Kay and a fellow named Buckley.

Mr. Banks and Kay reached the rear pews. He would have continued, but she held him back. "Hold it, Pops," she murmured. With the calmness of a general watching his forces deploy into battle, she stood poised, awaiting the proper moment.

The maid of honor was twenty feet ahead when he felt the gentle pressure of her arm. The stage was set as she wished it. She was ready for her entrance.

Out of the corners of his eyes Mr.

Banks caught glimpses of familiar faces. Their expression paid tribute to the girl at his side. Pride dispelled all other emotions.

He saw Buckley and the best man waiting for them at the end of the aisle. Mr. Galsworthy stood on the chancel steps smiling ever so slightly.

Now they were lined up before the steps and the minister was reading from a white satin book with a purple marker hanging from it.

When Mr. Galsworthy reached the place where he asked, "Who giveth this woman — ?" Mr. Banks was to say, "I do." It was his only line in the show. He wanted to acquit himself creditably and began to consider his delivery.

Should he say, "*I* do" or "I *do*"? "*I* do" sounded silly. It implied that any number of people might do it and that he was pushing himself forward for the job.

On the other hand "I *do*" didn't make much sense either. It certainly wasn't the proper way to answer a general question. The whole passage struck him as fatuous.

"Who giveth this woman — ?" intoned the rich baritone of the Reverend Mr. Galsworthy from far above him.

It caught him off guard in spite of all precautions. Kay nudged him and placed her hand in his. "*I* do," he murmured almost inaudibly, and passed her hand to Buckley. As he performed the simple act he was conscious that something deep within him ripped slightly.

He did not see the rest. Turning slowly, he stared defiantly at the rows of faces, then entered the first pew and stood beside Mrs. Banks. He tried in vain to listen to the words of the service — and then suddenly it was all over.

Kay beamed at them happily as she went by, her arm through Buckley's, and again Mr. Banks felt that queer little rending in the center of his being....

"Stanley, your hat looks like a cat in a thunderstorm," said Mrs. Banks as they descended the entrance steps of the church. "But it was lovely, darling, wasn't it?

Tallulah Bankhead:

MY BEAU IDEAL

In her autobiography Tallulah Bankhead writes of her hero — her "beau ideal."

Daddy, graduate of two colleges, used to say: "If you know your Bible, Shakespeare, and can shoot craps, you have a liberal education." To me he was a fusion of Santa Claus, Galahad, D'Artagnan and Demosthenes. He was the gallant, the romantic, the poet, above all the actor.

I can still quote yards of verse just from hearing him recite: "Hiawatha," "Little Orphan Annie," "The Spell of the Yukon," Cardinal Wolsey crying out: "had I but served my God with half the zeal I served my King, he would not in my age have left me naked to mine enemies." When he launched into "For God's sake, let us sit upon the ground and tell sad stories of the death of kings," he was Shakespeare's Richard II. His stories of Samson and Delilah, of Desdemona and Othello, were as exciting as *The Perils of Pauline.* He never read the Bible to us. He would tell us Biblical tales in his own words. He believed the whale swallowed Jonah, never wavered in his faith.

As vital to Daddy as food and drink was a forum, a stage, a pulpit. A skilled conversationalist, a born story-teller, a gentleman who rejoiced in rolling sentences and rococo rhetoric, he could have been another Edwin Booth (his profile was not unlike Booth's), another Billy Sunday, another William Jennings Bryan. He might even have been a dramatic critic. His journal has many pithy comments on plays he saw in New York.

Since Daddy needed a rostrum, he joined Tammany Hall. He was an active campaigner for Robert Van Wyck, candidate for mayor of New York. From cart tails in Chinatown and the Bowery he spoke for Van Wyck, lashed his opponent with Southern scorn.

Then another forum beckoned. An advertisement in a theatrical weekly stated young actors might find employment in a Boston stock company. Daddy applied forthwith, inventing a considerable professional past. To his joy and astonishment, he was told to report for rehearsal. Report he did, first writing Grandmother of his change of base and profession. He had just started to rehearse when he received a letter from Grandmother. He knew its contents. He went through what was to be his last stage drill, then crept away to a bench on the Common. He was to tell me years afterward that had it been a warmer day he might have flouted authority, stuck it out. But the chill of winter was in the air, he was broke, and his clothes were thin. He opened Grandmother's letter. As he suspected, she vetoed his theatrical career.

Years later when I was in Washington with a play and Daddy was Speaker of the House, he drove me to the stage door one night. As we parted he said, "Oh, Tallulah, if I had only had one whack at it!"

Do you see why Daddy was my hero? My beau ideal?

Nikos Kazantzakis:

ELEMENTARY SCHOOL

The literary giant from Crete, Nikos Kazantzakis, wrote "To my father's ferocious pedagogy I owe the endurance and obstinacy which have always stood by me in times of difficulty." Here, in his autobiography Report to Greco, *Kazantzakis describes how his father took him to school.*

With my ever-magic eye, my buzzing bee and honey-filled mind, a red woolen cap on my head and sandals with red pompons on my feet, I set out one morning, half delighted, half dismayed. My father held me by the hand; my mother had given me a sprig of basil (I was supposed to gain courage by smelling it) and hung my golden baptismal cross around my neck.

"God's blessings upon you, and my blessings too," she murmured, looking at me proudly.

I was like a small sacrificial victim

weighted down with ornaments. Within me I felt both pride and fear, but my hand was wedged deeply in my father's grasp, and I bore myself with manly courage. We marched and marched through the narrow lanes, reached Saint Minas's, turned, and entered an old building with a wide courtyard. Four great rooms occupied the corners and a dust-covered plane tree the middle. I hesitated, turning coward; my hand had begun to tremble in the large warm palm.

Bending over, my father touched my hair and patted me. I gave a start, for as far as I could remember, this was the first time he had ever caressed me. Lifting my eyes, I glanced at him fearfully. He saw that I was afraid and withdrew his hand.

"You're going to learn to read and write here so you can become a man," he said. "Cross yourself."

The teacher appeared in the doorway. He was holding a long switch and seemed like a savage to me, a savage with huge fangs. I pinned my eyes on the top of his head to see if he had horns. But I

was unable to see, because he was wearing a hat.

"This is my son," my father said.

Untangling my hand from his own, he turned me over to the teacher.

"His bones are mine, his flesh is yours. Don't feel sorry for him. Thrash him and make a man of him."

Upton Sinclair:

WHAT I GOT FROM

MY FATHER

As I think it over, I am inclined to say that what I got from my father was idealism. Although he had to live among the Yankees, he thought of himself as an old-fashioned Southern gentleman, and he lived up to old-fashioned ideals of honor and courtesy. There was something very quixotic about it, but it had a fine flavor of sentiment which I think I imbibed through the skin, as it were.

Clarence Day:

THE MUSIC LESSON

In Life With Father, *Clarence Day re-calls his father's attempt to teach him to sing — a frustrating episode born of the father's desire to see his son proficient in all things.*

One day when I was about ten years old, and George eight, Father suddenly re-membered an intention of his to have us taught music.... He held that all chil-dren should be taught to play on some-thing, and sing.

He was right, perhaps. At any rate, there is a great deal to be said for his program. On the other hand, there are children and children. I had no ear for music.

Father was the last man to take this into consideration, however: he looked upon children as raw material that a father should mold. When I said I couldn't sing, he said nonsense. He went to the piano. He played a scale, cleared his throat, and sang *Do, re, mi,* and the rest. He did this with relish. He sang it again, high and low. He then turned to me and told me to sing it, too, while he accompanied me.

I planted myself respectfully before him. He played the first note. He never wasted time in explanations; that was not his way; and I had only the dimmest understanding of what he wished me to do. But I struck out, haphazard, and chanted the extraordinary syllables loudly.

"No, no, no!" said Father, disgustedly.

At the end of what seemed to me an hour, I still stood at attention, while Father still tried energetically to force me to sing. It was an absolute deadlock. He wouldn't give in, and I couldn't.

Father finally gives up, and later...

He lit his cigar after dinner and leaned back philosophically, taking deep vigorous puffs with enjoyment, and drinking black coffee. When I said, "Good night, Father," he smiled at me like a

humorous potter, pausing to consider —
for the moment — an odd bit of clay. Then
he patted me affectionately on the shoul-
der and I went up to bed.

Richard Armour:

INNOCENT BYSTANDER

My little daughter loves to stand
   Beside me when I shave,
And, conscious of my gallery,
   I'm careful to behave.

She loves to see the lather foam,
   To hear the razor scrape.
She loves the way I screw my face
   In each unlovely shape.

She's spellbound by the gear I spread
   Upon the bathroom shelf,
But most of all she waits around
   In hopes I'll cut myself.

Herbert Gold:

PROBLEM SOLVING

Fathers are called upon to solve just about every problem, and they usually do. Sometimes, as in this selection from Herbert Gold's Fathers, even a father with the self-confidence of a Sam Gold can't cope with the situation. When his pregnant wife Frieda drives the family car — a Peerless — almost off the edge of a dock, Sam comes to the rescue.

At last my father arrived, still wearing his apron from the store. Lord of this lady, he set up his standard with a trumpet flourish, blowing his nose ferociously and saying, "What's the matter with you, kotchka?" in a voice fierce enough to put the terror into my mother and shiver the spines of a sympathetic audience. But his wounded gaze found him little different from her lounging Hungarian adviser.

"So you have to yell the machine back up?" she asked. "Shame, Sam, shame. I got the morning sickness again."

"What's the matter with you?" he added more gently. An inexperienced man in the back room of the store was pinching and lining the strawberry pint boxes. And who was to prevent the clerks from filling their pockets? His impatience needed forgiveness from her, even in her hour of need. "Kotchka" means "duckling."

The Hungarian tried to explain, repenting his earlier harshness, that hers was a mistake which anyone could make. My father did not believe this. "What's the matter with you?" he demanded while the Peerless wobbled.

"What's the matter with you?" he repeated softly, merely considering and judging, murmuring it contemplatively

this time, turning to measure the car and its predicament with a shrewd independent eye — that eye which was capable of challenging the A & P to do battle. My mother trembled with shame and love.

"All right, I'll drive it out," he announced.

A few splinters of applause in the springtime air of the Cuyahoga valley. "What?" demanded the duckling. It was her turn to be contemptuous. "You want to be a hero? Now it's your turn for crazy nuts?"

Opening the door stealthily so that no vibration could precipitate disaster, my father slid in behind the wheel. A hush descended over the Hungarian, the sailor, the crowd, and the children running in little circles at the edges of it. My mother, gasping, weakened by unspoken reproach, measured the brief allowance of wet splinters and blighted wood already under the front wheels.

She hadn't allowed him much.

He worked the starter. The Peerless motor made its truculent noise. He tightened the brakes and eased the gears into reverse. The brake too firm, he paused with a patient and masterful shrug of his heavy shoulders, full of wider considerations. The apron and the blue brawn of flesh at his arms distracted the watchers from the quick decision of his hands at the gearshift. He let out the brake slightly; with this motion, the clutch disengaged, and the gears slipping from reverse into neutral, the car jerked forward an inch or two. *Forward!* "Sam!" my mother cried. He came hurtling out the door, already angrily arguing, as the pilings cracked and splintered.

"Ah-hah, you see what you did?" he yelled. "It ain't enough you put the Peerless here, you had to—"

"But I didn't say anything! I didn't do anything, Sam. You—!"

While they shouted at each other, the automobile ponderously slid, thus resolving their discussion on the level of tragic action while the crowd breathed *Ahhh* in chorus. With just a groaning noise and then a crunching one, it leaned gracefully over the oily water; it plopped in; it could not swim toward the opposite shore; it settled helplessly with a gurgle and rush into the ooze.

Everyone watched, turning from the drowned car below the crippled dock to the fight between my father, gesticulating furiously, and my mother, stubborn, righteous, and scornful. The Hungarian, like most philanthropists not understanding all the issues, tried without success to mediate between the two of them. United in disaster, they turned coolly from him. "Kotch," my father said softly, holding her hand. Thus purged of pity and fear, as Aristotle remarks, my father called up his insurance man to find out how long he would have to wait until Metropolitan Auto & Life paid off.

Later the car was brought up, smelly and dripping; I think I was born the next week. Both events, I claim, were actions of my father's deliberation.

Captain Franz Jevne III:

FROM A DAD TO HIS DAUGHTER

ON HER FIRST BIRTHDAY

I cannot see across the miles
The lights, and bows,
  and birthday smiles
Just one dim night flare floats above
To mark the end of one year's love.

One year—too young to understand
Of flags, and men in far-off lands,
The grip of time on nations' wills,
Or hearts lost in these sad green hills.

But dreams can travel worlds away,
And in my heart I'll share this day.
A father's love will let me hold
My birthday angel, one year old.

(Written in Danang, South Vietnam)

Carl Sandburg:

A FATHER SEES HIS SON

A father sees a son nearing manhood.
What shall he tell that son? "Life is hard;
be steel; be a rock." And this might stand
him for the storms and serve him for
humdrum and monotony and guide him
amid sudden betrayals and tighten him
for slack moments. "Life is a soft loam;
be gentle; go easy." And this too might
serve him. Brutes have been gentled
where lashes failed. The growth of a
frail flower in a path up has sometimes
shattered and split a rock. A tough will
counts. So does desire. So does a rich
soft wanting. Without rich wanting nothing arrives. Tell him too much money
has killed men and left them dead years
before burial: the quest of lucre beyond a
few easy needs has twisted good enough
men sometimes into dry thwarted
worms. Tell him time as a stuff can be
wasted. Tell him to be a fool every so
often and to have no shame over having

been a fool yet learning something out of every folly hoping to repeat none of the cheap follies thus arriving at intimate understanding of a world numbering many fools. Tell him to be alone often and get at himself and above all tell himself no lies about himself whatever the white lies and protective fronts he may use amongst other people. Tell him solitude is creative if he is strong and the final decisions are made in silent rooms. Tell him to be different from other people if it comes natural and easy being different. Let him have lazy days seeking his deeper motives. Let him seek deep for where he is a born natural. Then he may understand Shakespeare and the Wright brothers, Pasteur, Pavlov, Michael Faraday and free imaginations bringing changes into a world resenting change. He will be lonely enough to have time for the work he knows as his own.

Henry Gregor Felson:

SHAKEDOWN CRUISE

Henry Gregor Felson, author of many books for young people, enlightens a difficult relationship in the following excerpt from his collection, Letters To A Teenage Son.

You know, when a new ship is built, it always goes through a series of shake-down cruises before it is assigned to active, equal duty with the fleet. The ship is taken out to sea and run through every possible beam-wracking and engine-cracking maneuver. Emergencies of every kind are simulated, and every effort is made to discover, before the ship is committed to action, all flaws in the construction and handling of the ship, and in the ability of the commander and crew.

I suppose adolescence could be described as the time of our human shake-down cruises. A time when we shove off in an untried ship manned by a green crew to make short, violent practice runs in the safety of our home waters.

You are engaged in your final series of shakedown runs. This is your last chance to practice, without serious risk, being independent and grown-up. It is your last chance to claim, simultaneously, the privileges of an adult and the responsibilities of a child. It is your last chance to be a man in every way possible for a boy to be.

It used to irritate me to see you reject my love, sneer at my ideals, scoff at my counsel, oppose my wishes — yet make all kinds of extravagant demands on me for service and purchases. I did not understand that the shakedown cruise often tests a few selected areas at a time.

When it was time for you to reject my love and friendship, it was also necessary to demand more money, more things, more favors, more "proof" that I loved you during the test. And I have noticed that when you want to stand on your own feet economically, and make very few "things" requests of me, you

are your most affectionate and companionable with me.

This need to prove your seaworthiness by fighting with me and rejecting me is transient, but it is not a game. Unless the emotions are real, the test is worthless. Honest heartache and genuine tears are the price we pay for your ticket to manhood. But it is a small price compared to what we would have to pay for peace during adolescence—your future manhood itself.

Carl B. Stokes:

THE DECIDING VOTE

Carl B. Stokes was the first Negro to be elected mayor of a major U.S. city. In November, 1969, the voters of Cleveland, Ohio, demonstrated their enthusiasm by returning him to the office for a second term. But he almost didn't run. In the following account, he tells how he arrived at the decision to seek another term.

My son, Carl, knows a lot about politics. He's just eleven, but we talk politics regularly and I take him with me to political meetings as often as I can. Carl understands the disillusionment, frustration and despair that a mayor sometimes feels. He knows how political life can drain a man of energy and he knows about the abuse a mayor must accept. Carl has heard the vicious, ugly names that disgruntled people have called me.

A politician's son must at times take abuse, too. Carl was nine at the time of my first campaign for mayor and he'd just started at a private school in Cleveland. It was a very conservative school and almost every youngster there was rooting for my opponent. Carl learned about direct abuse then.

He came home from school the first day with a question for his mother. "What's a nigger?" he asked.

Shirley explained. Then she asked why he'd inquired.

"That's what a boy in school called me," he told her.

"What did you say to him?" Shirley wanted to know.

"I said my name isn't Nigger, it's Carl."

There were other incidents of name-calling. Carl was a miserable little boy by the close of that campaign.

I had many doubts about running for re-election as the time came to decide. I felt a real hunger to return to private life, and Carl knew it. One evening that spring, I took him with me to a political banquet. On the way, he posed a direct question: "Daddy, are you going to run again?"

My son's opinion is very important to me. I knew how much he wanted a full-time, not a part-time, father. "Well, Carl, what do *you* think I should do?" I said.

His reply: "I think you should run. I think you're doing a pretty good job."

"You're aware that the kids may be very nasty to you again," I warned.

"I can take it if you can, Daddy," he said.

That was the moment I decided to run again. I should add that Carl has made up his mind not to go into politics. He says he wouldn't be a mayor for anything.

M. R. Hurley: HELPING DAD

My boy likes to sleep late
But he'd get up at dawn
To help me fix something
Or mow the lawn.

And many's the time
I've been tempted to say,
"Thanks, Son, but you'd only
Be in the way."

Then I stop and recall
That when I was a lad
The thing I loved most
Was helping my dad.

No matter the task,
He'd let me "help" do it,
And though small help or none
Well, I never knew it.

So I let my son help me
And praise what he does,
Trying to be half the dad
My father was.

William Allen White:

MARY WHITE

William Allen White's famous obituary for his daughter Mary has been published countless times since she died in 1921. A few paragraphs in White's autobiography, which discuss the obituary, are less well known, but no less a father's tribute.

The town was deeply moved by it. I could tell that. As I walked about I could see in the faces of people, even without their telling me, how the editorial about Mary had touched them. In a day or two, of course, the town forgot the editorial. Then the *Kansas City Star* picked it up. And Franklin P. Adams reprinted it in his "Conning Tower" in the *New York Tribune*. From there it went through the daily press of the country. And then a woman's magazine repeated it, then another and another. Christopher Morley was making an anthology and asked to include it. Alexander Woollcott put it into his first "Reader" and read it over the radio. Other radio entertainers used it and within a year it appeared in four books of reading for high schools and colleges.

Mary had been entered at Wellesley before her death; and in 1926, which would have been her graduating year, her class adopted her and dedicated the Wellesley Annual to her. She was carried on the rolls of the class of 1926 for many years. In the meantime, year after year, the piece appeared in innumerable anthologies. We kept tally on it for twenty years and it had been in more than forty of those school readers or anthologies of Americana, in the best of them and in the humbler ones. It has been a comfort to her mother and me to know that for a decade, at least, Mary will survive. She would now be in her forties. If the article never appeared in another book, she would survive in the hearts of youth well into her fifties. Hardly a day, never a week, passes that boys and girls in high schools and colleges do not write to me about "Mary."

Teachers often write, and whole classes sometimes join in a letter to her mother and me about her. The youth of today will remember her well into their maturity. She has a certain extension of her life in the lives of others. She survives, I think, as she would like to survive — in the hearts of her kind, high-school and college students. It is a strange immortality. Probably if anything I have written in these long, happy years that I have been earning my living by writing, if anything survives more than a decade beyond my life's span, it will be the thousand words or so that I hammered out on my typewriter that bright May morning under the shadow and in the agony of Mary's death. Maybe — when one thinks of the marvels of this world, the strange new things that man has discovered about himself and his universe, it could well be true — maybe in some distant world among the millions that whirl about our universe, Mary will meet her mother and me and, just as she grinned and looked up at her mother that evening when we climbed the

mountain in Colorado, with her hand
around my finger, she will grin:

"Daddy and I have had an adventure!"
It would be a gay and happy meeting.

Christopher Morley:

SECRET LAUGHTER

There is a secret laughter
                    That often comes to me,
And though I go about my work
                    As humble as can be,
There is no prince or prelate
                    I envy — no, not one.
No evil can befall me —
                    By God, I have a son!

Jean Renoir:

A FATHER'S LOVE

In 1915 Jean Renoir was sent to Paris to recuperate from war injuries. His father, the famous French Impressionist, then 73, was also brought to Paris to be near his son. In Renoir, My Father, *Jean describes their reunion.*

It was one of his models, La Boulangère, as we called her, who opened the door. She let out a shriek when she saw my crutches. Then Grand' Louise, our cook, appeared from my father's studio, which was on the same floor as our apartment. They both kissed me, and told me that "the boss" was busy painting some roses La Boulangère had bought on the Boulevard Rochechouart. I had noticed the flower woman leaning against the wheel of her little pushcart as I got out of the taxi. She was the very same one who had been there before the war. Outwardly nothing had changed, except that the rumble of cannon fire could be heard

when the wind was in the north.

My father was waiting for me in his wheel chair. For several years he had not been able to walk. I found him much more shrunken than when I had first left for the Front. Yet the expression on his face was as lively as ever. He had heard me out on the landing, and he was beaming with happiness, in which, however, there was a touch of irony. His eyes seemed to be saying, "They missed you this time, didn't they?" He handed his palette to Grand' Louise with an almost casual gesture, and warned me, "Mind you don't slip. The concierge waxed the floor in your honor, and it's very dangerous!" Turning to the two women, he said, "Wash it off well with plenty of water. Jean might slip and fall."

I kissed my father. His beard was wet with tears.

Richard J. Whalen:

THE FOUNDING FATHER

In his book The Founding Father, *Richard J. Whalen describes some parental ways of Joseph P. Kennedy, father of a distinguished American family:*

In the twentieth report of the Harvard Class of '12, published in 1932, he [Joseph P. Kennedy] gave his occupation as "capitalist." This was a bare description for a man perpetually in motion, an entrepreneur who plunged into situations promising wealth and prestige and pulled out quickly when the possibilities were exhausted. Nowhere, it seemed, did he leave a clue to his underlying purpose. Within the tight circle of Kennedys, however, he came literally and figuratively to rest, revealing that the only occupation to which he ever committed himself was fatherhood.... Of his children Kennedy once remarked: "No interest of mine is as great an interest as my interest in them."

"Little things are important," Kennedy told a reporter some years ago. "When Jack and Joe were just kids, when they were in a baseball or football game, or when the girls were in a school play, no matter where I was, Washington or the West Coast or wherever, and no matter how busy I was, I'd somehow get back to see them perform. That way they know you are interested, really interested, and when you tell them something it means something."

Kennedy may have exaggerated the details, there being no evidence that he ever took a train ride from California merely to please a child; but he certainly did not exaggerate the impact of his words on the children. When he spoke, they listened and obeyed.

As limited as it was, the time he spent with the children was exclusively theirs.

While he showed Jack a fine point of sailing, or taught Bobby how to grip a football, or held little Jean in the pool while she practiced the scissors kick, his work was forgotten and nothing less than a call from the President could interrupt.

Inauguration Day [Jan. 20, 1961] was dazzling bright and bitter cold.... Joe Kennedy [aged 72], ruddy-cheeked and beaming, wore a cutaway coat, put aside twenty-one years earlier when his ambassadorship ended; it had been a source of satisfaction to him that the coat needed no alteration.... In a relatively brief address containing passages of soaring eloquence, the youngest man ever elected to the Presidency proclaimed to the world that the torch of freedom had been passed to a new generation of Americans, "born in this century, tempered by war, disciplined by a hard and bitter peace, proud of our ancient heritage...." The next morning's newspapers would report that throughout the ceremony tears had glistened in Joe Kennedy's eyes.

Frederic Van de Water:

BRINGING UP FATHER

In his book Fathers Are Funny *Frederic Van de Water relates to his grown-up son his own reformation.*

When you were nine, I was a shabby, falsely pretentious rather comic person, beset by many problems of which I knew little, painfully eager to give my son a far better training than I possibly could, willing for that son's edification to pose at any moment and on the briefest notice in any inspiring attitude I might contrive. I was, in brief, a pretty average father.

So am I still, but any male parent who works at his job is bound to be somewhat more praiseworthy when his son is twenty than he was when the boy was nine. I am, for one thing, less of a hypocrite now than I was then. I dissembled shamefully in your earlier years, but I felt abashed when I did so and after each implicit fraud I did all that I could to justify my pretense by personal reform.

I improved, for one thing, in long division. I no longer lay slothfully in bed, mornings. I got up briskly as an example for you.

You made your toilet and got ready for school with a chaotic deliberation. The philippics I launched against this weakness impelled me to dress faster, myself. By the same system of belated reform I acquired other virtues, too.

Besides actually starting my work when I said I was going to and expurgating my speech and standing up when women entered the room, I didn't leave my spoon in my cup any longer. I folded my napkin after every meal. I was politer over the telephone. Because you habitually looked as though your clothes had been blown over you by a hurricane, and I spoke to you about it scathingly, I began to take more care about my own costume. I hung up my overcoat when I came in. I put my towel back where it belonged after use. I wiped out the tub when I had had my bath and restored books when I had finished with them to their proper place on the shelves.

Some of these excellences have fallen from me since you went away to school. Others have become permanent habits. If your childhood had endured for a dozen more years I should have been so thoroughly reconstructed by then that I should have looked forward, serenely, to the ultimate future, certain that I had qualified for a halo or, at the very least, a niche in the Hall of Fame.

William B. Franklin:

DEFINITION OF A DAD

If he's wealthy and prominent, and you stand in awe of him, call him "father." If he sits in his shirt sleeves and suspenders at a ball game and picnic, call him "Pop." If he wheels the baby carriage and carries bundles meekly, call him "Papa"—(with the accent on the first syllable). If he belongs to a literary circle and writes cultured papers, call him "Papa"—(with the accent on the last syllable).

If, however, he makes a pal of you when you're good, and is too wise to let you pull the wool over his loving eyes when you're not; if, moreover, you're sure no other fellow you know has quite so fine a father, you may call him "Dad."

Katherine Edelman:

PRIDE OF OWNERSHIP

My farmer father has love of land;
He often would reach
$\qquad$his lean brown hand,
Curving his fingers to form a cup,
And draw a handful of rich soil up.
I still can hear him, pride in his tone,
"Be rightly proud of the land you own."
Then, while brown earth
$\qquad$from his fingers spilled
Downward to furrows carefully tilled,
He would say —
$\qquad$his own wide fields in view —
"Keep the land, and the land
$\qquad$will keep you."

Edmund S. Muskie:

NO CHIP OFF THIS BLOCK

Maine's Senator Edmund S. Muskie became a popular national figure when he ran as the Democratic vice presidential candidate in 1968. The Muskies have five children. Stephen is the eldest.

Steve can work hard when he wants to. During the 1968 presidential campaign, he was assistant baggage manager, lugging heavy trunks and suitcases back and forth from airports to hotels. He put in fourteen- and sixteen-hour days, and he never let up. I was very impressed with him.

But I hadn't been so impressed with him at the end of his first semester at the University of Maine. His grades were terrible.

There were some understandable reasons for Steve's poor showing. Like many young people in college today, he felt uninvolved. He was deeply concerned

with the crucial problems of the day —
domestic and international — and most
of his courses had no bearing on those
problems. He challenged the existence
of the courses, and didn't study very
hard for them.

Fortunately, Steve agreed that his feel-
ings were no cause for low grades. Not
if he wanted to graduate. He promised
to do better.

At the next marking period, Steve
came to see me with his grades. They
were much higher than before, and he
was very proud of them.

I felt, though, that he could do still
better. I wondered whether I should
prod him. He might resent it, I knew.

"You don't seem very pleased," Steve
said.

I could tell he was angry. "Is this the
best you can do?" I asked.

He was quiet for a moment, thinking
it over. Probably thinking I was an awful
square. Then he said, firmly, "No, it
isn't, Dad. I can top this."

"Try," I urged.

He did. And at the end of the year, all

his grades were up. Except one. Steve flunked a course in public speaking. Can you imagine, a senator's son flunking public speaking! Obviously, Steve had heard too much of it at home.

Doris Chalma Brock:

INVENTORY OF DADDIES

Daddies have the tools to make
A doghouse or a kite,
Arms to swing you in the air
And hug you very tight.
Lots of games to play with you,
Experiments to try,
Dimes to give the ice cream man
When he comes whistling by.
Pocket knives and fishing rods,
A funny joke to share,
Hands to help with buttons, and
To fold with yours in prayer.

Composed in Melior,
a unique type face
designed by Hermann Zapf.
Printed on Hallmark
Eggshell Book paper.